REPORT VII (1)

International Labour Conference

THIRTY-FOURTH SESSION
1951

EQUAL REMUNERATION FOR MEN AND WOMEN WORKERS FOR WORK OF EQUAL VALUE

Seventh Item on the Agenda

GENEVA
International Labour Office
1950

331.2

PRINTED BY " IMPRIMERIES RÉUNIES S.A. ", LAUSANNE (SWITZERLAND)

CONTENTS

Page

INTRODUCTION 1

CHAPTER I : *Proceedings of the 33rd Session of the Conference relating to Equal Remuneration for Men and Women Workers for Work of Equal Value* 3

Extracts from the Report of the Conference Committee 3

Discussion in the Plenary Sitting of the Conference 38

CHAPTER II : *Proposed Texts* 48

I. *Texts for Consideration by the Conference Should it Decide to Adopt a Convention Supplemented by a Recommendation* . . . 52

  A. Proposed Convention concerning Equal Remuneration for Men and Women Workers for Work of Equal Value . . 52

  B. Proposed Recommendation concerning Equal Remuneration for Men and Women Workers for Work of Equal Value 54

II. *Text for Consideration by the Conference Should it Decide to Adopt a Recommendation Alone* 57

  Proposed Recommendation concerning Equal Remuneration for Men and Women Workers for Work of Equal Value 57

INTRODUCTION

On 30 June 1950, the International Labour Conference, meeting in its 33rd Session at Geneva, adopted the following Resolution by 117 votes to nil with 21 abstentions :

The Conference,

Having approved the report of the Committee appointed to examine item V on its agenda,

Having in particular approved as general conclusions, with a view to the consultation of Governments proposals for a Convention and/or a Recommendation relating to equal remuneration for men and women workers for work of equal value,

Decides to place on the agenda of its next general session the question of equal remuneration for men and women workers for work of equal value with a view to final decision on a Convention and/or a Recommendation on the subject.

In accordance with Article 39, paragraph 6, of the Standing Orders of the Conference concerning the double-discussion procedure, the Office is required to prepare one or more Conventions or Recommendations and to communicate them to Governments so as to reach them not later than two months from the closing of the session of the Conference, asking them to state within three months whether they have any amendments to suggest or comments to make.

The purpose of the present report is to transmit these texts to the Governments for their amendments or comments. The texts, which consist of a Convention supplemented by a Recommendation, and of a Recommendation alone, relating to equal remuneration for men and women workers for work of equal value, are based on the conclusions adopted by the Conference at its 33rd Session, which included the Resolution reproduced above.

The decisions reached by the International Labour Organisation between 1919 and 1950 regarding the principle of equal remuneration for men and women workers for work of equal value, as well as the present legislation and practice of the different countries in this regard, have already been reviewed in Report V (1) prepared for the 33rd Session of the Conference.[1]

---

[1] International Labour Conference, 33rd Session, Geneva, 1950, Report V (1): *Equal Remuneration for Men and Women Workers for Work of Equal Value* (Geneva, 1949).

In order that the Office may comply with time limits laid down by the Standing Orders of the Conference, Governments are urged to communicate their amendments or observations with regard to the texts now submitted to them as soon as possible, and in any case so that they may reach the Office not later than 15 December 1950. It is also suggested that Governments which have no amendments to propose or observations to make should inform the Office by the same date whether they consider the proposed texts constitute an adequate basis for discussion at the 34th Session of the Conference.

CHAPTER I

PROCEEDINGS OF THE 33rd SESSION OF THE CONFERENCE RELATING TO EQUAL REMUNERATION FOR MEN AND WOMEN WORKERS FOR WORK OF EQUAL VALUE

Extracts from the Report of the Conference Committee

The Committee on Equal Remuneration for Men and Women Workers for Work of Equal Value, which was set up by the International Labour Conference at its third sitting on 8 June 1950 to examine the fifth item on the agenda, was composed of 72 members (36 Government, 18 Employers' and 18 Workers' members). The Committee elected Sir Guildhaume Myrddin-Evans, Government member, United Kingdom, as Chairman ; Mr. Bergenström, Employers' member, Sweden, and Mr. Vermeulen, Workers' member, Netherlands, as Vice-Chairmen ; and Miss Miller, Government member, United States, as Reporter.

General Discussion

The Committee began its work with a general discussion, to which it devoted three sittings.

Speaking on behalf of the Employers' members, the Swedish Employers' member expressed the view that Reports V (1) and (2) should be examined before the proposed conclusions were considered. He questioned, for example, in Report V (1) the interpretation of the French legislation on equal remuneration for male and female workers and the statements made concerning the restrictions on the employment of women in night work. He pointed out that only 26 out of 61 States Members had replied in the affirmative to the question concerning the desirability of international regulations on equal remuneration, and that in many countries the employers did not share the views of their Governments on the question. It seemed impossible at this time to reach agreement on this matter which, more perhaps than any other, raised social, economic and financial problems varying from country to country. Existing procedures for fixing conditions of work varied greatly and in some countries both employers and workers attached great importance to preserving free collective bargaining, independent of State intervention. The question of equality of remuneration between men and women formed an integral part of the general question of wages. Further, the problem was complicated by other considerations, such as the relative strength of trade union organisation among men and women ; the relative demand for female labour ; the situation in countries which need to induce an expansion of exports ; and such human problems as the protection of the family. In view of these considerations, the Employers' members did not consider the subject as dealt with in Report V (2) was sufficiently understood to enable a decision to be taken as to whether the subject lent itself or not to international regulations. If the Office text were taken, the answer would definitely be in the negative. The Employers' members were, however, prepared to participate in a discussion to clarify the issue.

The Italian, French, Brazilian, Canadian, Turkish, New Zealand, Argentine, Indian, Swedish, Finnish, Mexican, United Kingdom, United States and Union of South Africa Government members in turn indicated the views of their Governments on the desirability of adopting international regulations on this question.

The Italian Government member stated that while his Government had not been able to reply to the questionnaire, it fully appreciated the economic and social importance of the question. The principle of equal remuneration was contained in the Italian Constitution. His Government favoured the adoption of a Convention supplemented by a Recommendation which would provide for the flexibility needed in methods of applying the principle in order to take account of the variety of economic and social conditions in different countries.

The French Government member stated that equality of remuneration had been established in France as regards all levels of minimum wages and that no particular difficulties had been encountered in the application of the Law of 30 July 1946. Agreeing that an allowed variation often existed as between the effective wages of men and women, he pointed out that a variation above the minimum existed also among men workers. This variation was based on the aptitudes, capacities, professional competence, etc., of the individuals concerned and not on differences in individual needs. The French Government member considered that the argument that wages were dependent upon the relative strength of collective bargaining agents was without validity, because it was unthinkable that the financial ability of an undertaking to pay wages was relative to the strength or weakness of trade unions. It had been found that equality of wage tended to reduce absenteeism, the sense of inferiority and discontent among women workers. He reaffirmed the support of the French Government for a Convention supplemented by a Recommendation.

The Brazilian Government member declared that he would support a Convention. The principle had already been widely acknowledged, and it would therefore be of little value merely to reaffirm it in a Recommendation which would have very little practical effect.

The Canadian Government member pointed out the need to reconcile two different methods of application, namely, by legal enactment and by collective agreements. While the existing text of points 4 and 5 of the proposed conclusions was not satisfactory as it stood, the Canadian Government and the provinces, all but one of which had replied to an enquiry on the subject, were in favour of the principle and of its application to State employees. They would not, however, be prepared to introduce legislation in this sphere.

The Turkish Government member expressed general approval of the proposals of the Office and stressed the importance of opportunities for promotion for women and the need to make certain that the costs of social services payable with respect to women should not be met by a reduction of women's wages. His Government favoured the adoption of a Convention and the application of the principle of equal remuneration by legislative action.

The New Zealand Government member approved the principle of equal remuneration but favoured the adoption of a Recommendation only. He stressed the need for further clarification of, and agreement upon, methods of application prior to the adoption of a Convention and the necessity of gradual application to avoid difficulties of a financial character and to take account of social and economic conditions. The relationship of the principle of the family wage, tax exemptions with respect to wife and children, and a comprehensive system of social security and family allowances, would need to be studied in New Zealand in relation to application of the principle of equal remuneration.

The Argentine Government member favoured the adoption of international regulations.

The Indian Government member favoured a Recommendation in view of the need for flexibility in methods of application and the difficulties in the technically less advanced countries of providing means of objective evaluation of " job content ", as proposed in the conclusions submitted by the Office. Wide discretion should be left to States Members.

The Swedish Government member noted that the subject of equal remuneration was closely bound up with questions of social policy, for which Governments were taking increasing responsibility. Despite doubts as to its feasibility, her Government was prepared to take part in an effort to reach international agreement upon this question. The Swedish Government, however, would favour a Recommendation only at this time, in such form as to take full account of the position in those countries, like Sweden, where wages were fixed by collective bargaining without intervention of the public authorities. Reports V (1) and (2) and the replies of 33 Governments to the questionnaire provided a basis for discussion.

The Finnish Government member called attention to the expansion of women's employment : in Finland, about 48 per cent. of the workers in industry, commerce and the public service were women. The difference between the wages of men and women was in the region of 10 to 20 per cent. In the public service, wages were fixed in accordance with work done, but women had less opportunity for advancement and held less well-paid posts. Although the question of equal remuneration for men and women was an integral part of the wages question, it would be unjust to seek lower costs of production by keeping down the level of women's wages. In Finland, with the provision of family allowances, tax exemptions and low-cost housing, the concept of a family wage was declining in importance. Social services such as maternity leave, nurseries, etc., were considered to be measures of social assistance ; they should not be financed by an indirect levy upon women's wages.

The Mexican Government member favoured a Convention covering general principles, supplemented by a Recommendation formulating methods of application. He called attention to the establishment of the principle of equal remuneration under the Mexican Constitution of 1917, and the provisions for application of the principle in the Federal Labour Code.

The United Kingdom Employers' member at this stage posed a series of questions, which had not yet been discussed. He asked :

" What exactly does the expression 'equal remuneration for men and women workers for work of equal value' mean ? What is meant by determining the relative value of labour and how far is it to be carried ? What is job content in relation to the value of work ? How does one reconcile the establishment of job content with collective bargaining ? Does equal remuneration imply equality of time rates ? Is it believed that the Government should be responsible for the application of the principle in industry, and if so, should the Government intervene in collective bargaining and in the establishment of job content ? How is family responsibility to be dealt with, which cannot be ignored despite the progress of general conditions ? What would be the effects of the application of a principle of equal pay on collective agreements concerning piece work, such as those in the United Kingdom ? These questions must be fully examined, either during the general discussion, or in connection with the various points in the text."

The United Kingdom Government member considered that the Committee should examine with care the complex problems of a practical character which arose in applying the principle of equal remuneration and should reach coherent and constructive conclusions that would be broadly applicable, even though conditions varied greatly from country to country.

The United Kingdom Government accepted in principle, as regards their own employees, the justice of the claim that there should be no difference in payment for the same work in respect of sex. They considered nevertheless that they could not apply this principle at the present time because they must take account of the financial and economic implications of equal remuneration in the public service and of the repercussions of such a measure on the various other branches of employment. The application of the principle had a close bearing on the structure and development of the social services. In considering the obligations which they were to assume under the proposed regulations, Governments could not avoid considering also the proportion of the national income which they were in a position to see devoted to social purposes generally. The conclusions reached by the Committee should indicate clearly that application of the principle of equal remuneration should take into account the social development and economic and financial conditions of the countries concerned.

In the view of the United Kingdom Government, the Committee should concentrate on what appeared to be the underlying principle of equal remuneration, namely, that there should be no discrimination in regard to remuneration which was based upon the sex of the worker. To introduce a concept of remuneration in accordance with job content would be to raise a number of almost insoluble problems. What criteria for the appraisal of job content could be found which would be applicable to all industries and professions ? Even if applied separately and in particular fields job evaluation required strict methods of analysis. It was not clear, however, what elements would be included in the appraisal of jobs or on what basis decisions would be reached on the relative rate to be accorded to each element. It appeared doubtful in any case whether remuneration generally would, in practice, be based exclusively on job content. Such procedures if generally applied might well lead to a rigidity of the industrial structure which would have undesirable economic effects.

Finally, in the opinion of the United Kingdom Government, the question of equal remuneration was one aspect of the general question of wages and it was not disposed to intervene in the process of wage fixing, even in nationalised sectors of the economy or where wages and salaries are fixed by statutory authorities. Points 4 and 5 of the text proposed by the Office provided that effect might be given to international regulations by means of collective agreements, but how could the Government of a highly industrialised country ensure that all collective agreements respected the principle ?

In view of all these problems, the United Kingdom Government proposed that points 2 to 8, inclusive, of the Office text should be replaced by another text (quoted in full below) which they offered to the Committee as a more effective basis of discussion.

The United States Government member reported that her Government approved the principle of equal remuneration and carried it out in practice. While the application of the principle raised many problems, the question could not be avoided. The development of world economy required the assistance of female labour. The numerical importance of women workers was such that their lower wages constituted a menace to the general level of wages.

Where the principle of equal remuneration was applied in the United States, agreements must require that women receive the same base rate and the same rate of premium, in relation to work performed, as men ; the rate must not differ because of sex. As regards the family wage, there did not need to be conflict with the principle of equal remuneration, so long as special supplements in respect of family or other dependants were paid to the worker irrespective of sex.

The Union of South Africa Government member emphasised the importance of maintaining the economic equilibrium of the country and freedom of collective bargaining. His Government had declined to take a definite decision as regards international regulations on the question of equal remuneration until the Committee had defined the principle. In any event, they would only favour a Recommendation.

The Netherlands Employers' member emphasised the relation of equal remuneration to cost of production ; in the opinion of the Netherlands employers, as of the International Organisation of Employers, female labour led to higher costs than male labour, even when the work performed was identical. Moreover, the proportion of the wage which was related to family need could not be related to the principle of equal remuneration. Only that element of the wage which corresponded to work performed could be so related in the opinion of the Netherlands employers, and the practical value of such an interpretation of the principle was doubtful.

The Australian Employers' member stated that he would like to make the position of those he represented quite clear. They were of the opinion that the very complex subject before this Committee was not capable of international regulation, but they did desire to make every contribution possible towards clarification of this subject now as it would have to be dealt with at future sessions of the International Labour Conference.

Finally, the United Kingdom Workers' member, speaking on behalf of the Workers' members, announced that most of the Workers' members favoured the adoption of a Convention even though they realised the difficulties of its application. She protested against the argument that human and social factors made it impracticable to apply the principle of equal remuneration, pointing out that the discontent of women workers and the injustice in their situation were also human problems requiring consideration. Experience in the United Kingdom, during and since the war, with collective agreements which included the principle of equal remuneration, demonstrated the feasibility of this method of application. She disagreed with the argument that application of the principle should be held in abeyance to give priority to the development of the social services, particularly since these were largely financed by Government, whereas wages were largely paid by private employers. The Workers' members therefore opposed the alternative draft which had been submitted by the United Kingdom Government member as a basis for discussion.

The Chairman thereupon closed the general discussion and asked whether the Committee wished to adopt as a basis for its discussions the proposed conclusions prepared by the Office in Report V (2) or the alternative draft offered by the United Kingdom Government member.

This draft included points 1 and 9 to 13 of the Office text and replaced points 2 to 8 by the following :

2. Remuneration should be regarded as including all the benefits and advantages, whether in cash or in kind, accruing to the worker in return for work done.

3. *(a)* In furtherance of the principle of equal remuneration for men and women workers for work of equal value, measures should be taken to promote the establishment of rates of remuneration without discrimination based on sex.

(b) Such measures should be appropriate to the established national procedures for determining rates of remuneration and should be decided in the light of the development of social policy and financial and economic circumstances of the country concerned.

4. Appropriate action should be taken in accordance with the terms of these regulations—

(a) to bring the provisions of these regulations to the notice of all wage and salary fixing authorities and employers' and workers' organisations concerned ;

(b) after consultation with the workers' organisations concerned, to ensure to the employees of the Government rates of remuneration determined in accordance with the principle set out in paragraph 3.

The Brazilian Government member urged the Committee to take a decision first on the form of the regulations, because it would be desirable that the general attitude on this subject should be made clear before undertaking discussion. He also proposed that the Committee should consider the text it wished to adopt as a basis of discussion before deciding upon the form of the regulations.

The United States Government member and the Belgian Government member considered that the adoption of this text as a basis for discussion would imply a decision as to the form of the international regulations since this text was not suitable for a Convention.

The Italian Government member, supported by the United Kingdom Workers' member, proposed that the conclusions prepared by the Office should be taken as a basis for discussion.

The Swedish Employers' member, speaking on behalf of the majority of the Employers' members, supported the United Kingdom Government member's proposals as a more realistic approach to the possibility of an international regulation on so complex a subject. He stated that the Employers' members would vote for the alternative text as a basis for discussion, though that would not commit them, either individually or collectively, on the substance of the problem.

The Australian Government member likewise supported the text of the United Kingdom Government member as a basis for discussion, stating that it avoided unnecessary detail while providing ample scope for the discussions of the Committee.

The alternative text was then put to the vote and was rejected as a basis for discussion by 40 votes to 49.

The Committee then decided to take the proposed conclusions prepared by the Office as the basis for its discussions.

The United Kingdom Employers' member, anxious to avoid any misunderstanding, desired to make it clear that if he voted for any particular text—either in the original or in an amended form—it would be with a view to helping the next session to understand more clearly than they did at the present time what they were trying to deal with. This must not be taken to mean that the United Kingdom employers considered such a text to be appropriate to an international regulation.

Proposed Conclusions [relating to International Regulations concerning Equal Remuneration for Men and Women Workers for Work of Equal Value

I. FORM OF THE INTERNATIONAL REGULATIONS

Point 1

On the decision of the Committee, the discussion on the form of the international regulations took place after the examination of points 2 to 13 of the conclusions proposed by the Office.

Seven Government members, including the representatives of the Argentine Republic, Belgium, Brazil, France, Italy, Mexico and Peru, spoke in favour of the adoption of Part II as a Convention supplemented by Part III as a Recommendation. The Israeli and Turkish Government members, as well as the Workers' members, also spoke generally in favour of a Convention supplemented by a Recommendation, while the French and Italian Employers' members opposed the adoption of both regulations for the specific reasons stated hereafter. Eight Government members, including the representatives of Australia, Canada, India, Indonesia, New Zealand, Sweden, Switzerland and the United Kingdom, and three Employers' members, representing the Belgian, United States and Uruguayan employers, favoured a Recommendation alone.

Two Government members, representing Australia and Switzerland, and two Employers' members, representing the Belgian and Uruguayan employers, were opposed to the adoption of a Convention.

The United States Government member stated that her Government, because of its structure, could not support a Convention on this subject at present. She reserved the right to vote in favour of whatever measure appeared to her best to further the aim of setting up standards for equal remuneration and the acceptance of these standards.

The Belgian, Brazilian, French and Italian Government members favoured a Convention supplemented by a Recommendation on the grounds that acceptance of the principle was widespread, that difficulties of application were not insuperable, that all economies could bear the cost of improvements in human conditions, and that application of the principle was not only politically sound but in accordance with the traditions of the I.L.O. They declared, however, that the Convention which they would wish to see adopted should allow for application progressively, flexibly, and by stages, to take into account the diversity of economic and social conditions in the various countries and thus to enable their economy to put the principle into operation without any ill effect. They therefore proposed at the outset that the Convention should embody " General Principles " and that " Methods of Application " should be included in a Recommendation.

The Israeli Government member proposed a Recommendation in addition to a Convention because it appeared from the discussions of the Committee that not all of the points would be appropriate for a Convention. The Turkish Government member, in support of both regulations, emphasised the need to protect countries applying the principle, particularly for the sake of their export trade. The Netherlands Workers' member, on behalf of the other Workers' members, supported the adoption of a Convention supplemented by a Recommendation, the regulations to permit progressive application on the basis of the compromise text in order to take into account the diversity of social and eco-

nomic situations of States Members, believing that the problems
of application would not be insuperable, and noting that the majority of Governments were in favour of the adoption of an international regulation. In view, however, of the differences of opinion,
he reserved the right of the Workers' members to move at a later
stage of the discussion the deferment of the decision to the next
session of the Conference.

The French Employers' member, while not objecting to a
clear and concise draft Convention, stated that he could not accept
any text of a Convention or of a Recommendation that would
include the provisions laid down in point 11, whether in the Office
text or the wording drawn up by the Committee, because in his
opinion these provisions permitted Government intervention in
job evaluation or other procedures involved in the application
of the principle. The Italian Employers' member opposed both
forms of regulations since point 3 did not define equal work in
terms of equal output. In addition, he agreed with the objection
of the French Employers' member.

The Swiss Government member favoured the adoption of a
Recommendation on the grounds that the principle of equality
and its practical application varied so greatly in the different
countries that it did not seem indicated at the present time that
the Committee should proceed directly to the adoption of international regulations in the form of a Convention. Furthermore,
there was no governmental intervention in the fixing of wages in
Switzerland in view of the economic and federal system prevailing
in this country.

The Belgian Employers' member and the New Zealand Government member believed that the adopted text, as it stood, would be
difficult to enforce as a Convention, and would be more workable
in the form of a Recommendation. The Indian and Indonesian
Government members preferred a Recommendation because do-
mestic conditions in their countries precluded the application of
a Convention on the subject at this time. The Swedish Government
member considered a Recommendation more appropriate because
several Governments were opposed to a Convention, notably on
account of their systems of wage fixing.

The United States employers believed in the principle, their
member stated, and favoured the adoption of a Recommendation.
Women workers were numerically important, industrially valuable,
in many cases had families fully dependent upon them or were
self-supporting, had the same costs of living, and in the interests

2

of mass production industry their purchasing power should be expanded.

The Uruguayan Employers' member stated he would support the adoption of a Recommendation for the following reasons : first, because the principle had not been defined in a satisfactory manner ; secondly, because the representatives of many Governments had declared that it would not be possible to ratify a Convention ; and thirdly because in a question of such importance it was necessary to proceed with extreme caution.

Finally, the Netherlands Workers' member, speaking on behalf of the other Workers' members and supported by the Belgian, Brazilian, French and Italian Government members, who had also proposed the adoption of both a Convention and a Recommendation, moved that a decision on the form of an international regulation should be deferred until the next session of the Conference, when there might be a greater measure of agreement on the question.

An amendment which sought to defer until the next session of the Conference decision as to the form of the international regulations, having been earlier proposed by the Employers' members on the understanding that point 1 would be considered immediately after Part II, was withdrawn by them when the matter was not brought up until after Part III. The amendment was then taken up again by the Workers' members, was put to the vote and was carried by 50 votes against 39, with 7 abstentions. This amendment provided for the preparation by the Office of alternative texts for *(a)* a Convention embodying principles, supplemented by a Recommendation concerning methods of application, and *(b)* a Recommendation on principles and on methods of application.

The United Kingdom Employers' member stated that the reason for his participation in the withdrawal of the Employers' amendment would be made clear at a later date.

The Chairman noted that in view of this decision the Office would have to prepare for next year alternative texts presenting Part II, General Principles, in the form of a Convention and of a Recommendation, and Part III, Methods of Application, in the form of a Recommendation.

II. General Principles

Point 2

The text proposed by the Office read as follows :

2. For the purpose of international regulation, the term " remuneration " to be defined as including wage or salary rates as well as the various bonuses or other allowances in cash or in kind, the seniority provisions and the system of wage payment established by the wage provisions covering the men and women workers concerned.

The Workers' members proposed that the following should be substituted for this text :

2. For the purpose of the international regulations, the term " remuneration " to be defined as including—

(a) the ordinary or basic wage or salary ; and

(b) any increment, supplement, margin, bonus, allowance or other addition to such ordinary or basic wage or salary, whether in cash or in kind.

The United States Government member proposed the addition, after " basic " in subparagraph (a) of this text, of the words " rate of " ; and the Belgian Government member proposed the addition, at the end of (b), of the words " and in general all that the worker receives in return for work done ". These amendments were accepted by the Workers' members, subject to (b) reading as follows : " and, in general, everything furnished to the worker for the work performed ".

A number of questions were raised with a view to clarification of the definition contained in this amendment. The Swedish and Uruguayan Employers' members opposed the idea that the system of increments based on seniority should be included in the system of remuneration for the purpose of equal remuneration, while the United Kingdom Employers' member did not believe that merit rates paid to workers for reasons not related to the value of their work for this purpose should be included in the definition.

At the request of the Italian Government member, it was made clear that no " allowance " made under a public system of social security should be considered as part of remuneration. Only allowances made directly by the employer should be considered to constitute part of remuneration.

The Netherlands Workers' member, speaking on behalf of the Workers' members, maintained that increments based on seniority were an integral part of the system of remuneration. He considered that individual merit bonuses should be granted in accordance with the same principles to workers of both sexes, and indicated that the allowances referred to in the amendment were those allowances which were paid under social security schemes financed by the undertaking or industry concerned and which thus formed a part of the system of remuneration in operation in such undertakings. The United States Government member considered that the definition of remuneration should include all those elements in wages which, by virtue of point 3 of the Office text, should not be subject to discrimination based upon sex.

The French Government member pointed out that equal remuneration for men and women involved equal minimum wage rates for men and women.

The United Kingdom Government member suggested the following alternative definition :

Remuneration should be regarded as including all the benefits and advantages, whether in cash or in kind, received by the worker from his employer in return for work done.

He withdrew this proposal in favour of the following revised text which was proposed as a compromise by the Workers' members:

For the purpose of international regulation, the term " remuneration " to be defined as including—

(a) the rate of ordinary, basic or minimum wage or salary ; and

(b) any additional emoluments whatsoever either in cash or in kind received by the worker from his employer and arising out of his employment.

The United Kingdom Employers' member took over the amendment which had been withdrawn by the United Kingdom Government member and moved it in the following modified form :

Remuneration for the purpose of " equal remuneration for men and women workers for work of equal value " should be defined as all the benefits and advantages, whether in cash or kind, received by the worker from his employer in return for the work done.

This proposal was rejected by 30 votes to 45 with 11 abstentions, and the Workers' members' revised amendment was adopted by 47 votes to 30 with 8 abstentions, replacing point 2 of the Office text.

Point 3

The Office text was as follows :

3. The phrase " equal remuneration for men and women workers for work of equal value " to be defined as meaning that remuneration

rates shall be established on the basis of job content, no discrimination being made on the basis of the sex of the worker.

Fourteen amendments were submitted to this point, of which four came to a vote, the rest being withdrawn.

The United Kingdom Government member moved an amendment which was supported by the Italian and New Zealand Government members and which, as modified on the proposal of the Australian Government member, proposed that the Office text should be replaced by the following :

In furtherance of the principle of equal remuneration for men and women workers for work of equal value, measures should be taken to promote the establishment of rates of remuneration without discrimination based on sex, and where necessary and appropriate for this purpose to facilitate objective comparison between the work performed by men and women workers engaged on comparable jobs, whether on the basis of job content or other suitable means.

The essential purpose of this amendment was, first, to make clear that the primary object of the international regulations should be to eliminate discrimination based on sex and, secondly to avoid making mandatory the use of job content or any other specified criterion as the basis for the comparison of work performed by men and women workers.

The Belgian Government member considered this wording too vague and difficult to apply.

The Indian Government member presented an amendment, which was seconded by the Canadian Government member and supported, after modification, by the United States Government member and the Workers' members. This amendment, as thus modified, proposed that the Office text be replaced by the following :

The phrase " equal remuneration for men and women workers for work of equal value " shall be defined as meaning that wage or salary rates shall be established on the basis of job content; but where that is not practicable, on any other basis as laid down by the competent authorities, provided that no discrimination shall be made on account of the sex of the worker.

This amendment was designed to retain the criterion of job content which a number of the members of the Committee desired and, at the same time, to provide for the use of alternative methods in countries in which job evaluation was not generally feasible. The Australian Government member considered however that this text went too far in requiring the use of the job content basis wherever "practicable", since even in such cases it might be desirable to make use of other criteria as well.

The amendments proposed by the United Kingdom Government member and the Indian Government member, together with a sub-amendment to the latter which had been proposed by the Israeli Government member, were all withdrawn in favour of the following compromise text proposed by the Government members of Australia, India, the United Kingdom and the United States :

3. (1) For purposes of these regulations, equal remuneration for men and women workers for work of equal value to be regarded as meaning that rates of remuneration shall be established without discrimination based on sex.

(2) Where necessary and appropriate for this purpose, measures to be taken to promote objective appraisal of jobs on the basis of job content or, if more suitable, any other basis as may be decided upon by the authorities or bodies responsible for the determination of remuneration.

This text was supported by the Workers' members, and was opposed by the United Kingdom Employers' member on the ground that it would involve extensive revision of existing collective agreements and statutory instruments laying down wage rates for women, and impossible negotiations as to the relative value of each job, and would provide an opening for new demands. The Italian Government member also opposed the amendment on the ground that it would be subject to varying interpretations in the different countries.

The Belgian, Brazilian, French, Italian, Mexican and Peruvian Government members proposed that the Office text be replaced by the following :

The phrase " equal remuneration for men and women workers for work of equal value " to be defined as meaning that equal remuneration, without distinction on the basis of sex, shall be paid for work of equal value performed for the same employer in the same locality or for duties which are identical, comparable and of equal value, and are performed for the same employer in the same locality. Differences in remuneration based on seniority are admissible, so long as supplements or additions paid in virtue of seniority or length of service as well as promotions are assured, under the same conditions, to both sexes.

This amendment was supplemented by the following, which proposed a definition of the expression " work of equal value " :

By " work of equal value " is meant work which yields the same output or productivity, in terms of quantity and quality, or which is performed by persons with the same professional or technical ability. In professions in which there is a regular hierarchy, workers of the same category or grade should be considered as performing work of equal value.

The Italian Government member and the Brazilian Employers' member withdrew their amendments to point 3 in favour of this jointly drafted text. The aim of the new amendment was to take into account, in establishing the principle of equal remuneration, the ideas of " same locality " and " same employer ", and to deal specifically with the question of differences in remuneration based on seniority.

The Italian and Scandinavian Employers' members withdrew amendments which they had previously proposed and joined with the rest of the Employers' members in support of a proposal that the Office text be replaced by the following :

The phrase " equal remuneration for men and women workers for work of equal value " to be defined as meaning that remuneration rates shall be established on the basis of quality, quantity (where appropriate) and other characteristics of the work performed and of the cost of production or service, no discrimination being made on the basis of the sex of the workers.

The purpose of this amendment was to provide that the value of the work should be measured in terms of its quality and quantity and also in terms of the costs of production, which were higher when women were employed and had to be taken into account if equal remuneration were not to increase the risk of unemployment for women. The Workers' members believed that the phrase " other characteristics of work done " provided a loophole, and did not consider that costs of production should be taken into account.

The Employers' members' amendment was rejected by 30 votes to 54 with 5 abstentions. The amendment of the Belgian, Brazilian, French, Italian, Mexican and Peruvian Government members was also rejected by 8 votes to 71 with 5 abstentions.

The Employers' members' amendment having been defeated, the Swedish Employers' member withdrew a similar amendment regarding production costs which he had proposed, without seeking a vote on it. The Committee then adopted by 51 votes to 31 with 8 abstentions the amendment proposed by the Government members of Australia, India, the United Kingdom and the United States, and rejected by 28 votes to 49 with 11 abstentions a proposal by the Netherlands Employers' member that the following words be added to this amendment :

Departure from the provisions of point 3 to be permitted in all cases where wage rates are fixed with reference to family needs. Such departure to be limited to the extent to which the family needs are justifiably taken into account.

The Workers' members had objected to the consideration of family needs in connection with equal remuneration as being irrelevant.

The amendment of the Belgian, Brazilian, French, Italian, Mexican and Peruvian Government members having been defeated, these members decided to withdraw a second amendment which would have constituted an additional point, following point 3 in the text, and which defined " work of equal value " in terms of quality and quantity of output produced by persons with the same professional or technical ability, workers in the same category or grade being considered as performing work of equal value.

The Committee then adopted point 3 as amended, the French text being subject to review by the Drafting Committee.

In this connection, as a result of discussions in the Drafting Committee, the Belgian Employers' member pointed out that the English expression " job content " did not appear to be capable of translation as " nature du travail ". The French-speaking and Spanish-speaking employers considered that it would be necessary to use here a periphrasis such as " valeur intrinsèque du travail en quantité et en qualité dans l'exercice d'une fonction déterminée ". If this question was merely one of form it would be resolved by the Drafting Committee ; if not, the Office should endeavour to formulate a sufficiently clear definition of the term " job content " so that in the future an accurate translation might be made.

Point 4

The text proposed by the Office read as follows :

4. Each Member to undertake to ensure, by means appropriate to procedures for fixing rates of remuneration which are in force in the country, the application of the principle of equal remuneration for men and women workers for work of equal value, or to satisfy itself that this principle is applied.

Three amendments were presented, one by the United Kingdom Government member, another by the Australian Government member and a third by the United States Government member. The United Kingdom Government member's amendment proposed that the Office text be replaced by the following :

Action taken in accordance with the preceding paragraph to be appropriate to the established national procedures for determining rates of remuneration, and to be decided in the light of the development of social policy and financial and economic circumstances of the countries concerned.

The United Kingdom Government member explained that the object of this amendment was to provide the necessary flexibility as to the nature and timing of the measures to be taken under the regulations. It was essential, in his view, that full account should be taken of the factors mentioned in the amendment. The amendment was seconded by the Indian Government member.

The United Kingdom Employers' member declared that the amendment seemed quite reasonable, although he doubted the practicability of an international regulation. Countries which had laboriously developed their social institutions could not be expected to compromise their social policy for the sake of an unknown quantity such as the equality of remuneration. In the course of collective bargaining, the question of family needs was still raised by the trade unions when discussing men's wages. When certain employers made reference to costs of production they had meant supplementary costs arising from the employment of female labour as compared with men, and it was clear that at least in some cases this addition to total costs was appreciable. The system of fixing wages according to job content is still in an elementary stage. The value attributed to the various elements of the work was arbitrary and subjective. Moreover, this method can and does provide lower levels of remuneration for work normally done by women. This method can be summarised as the rate for the job, which is already widely applied in the United Kingdom. It would be unwise to allow special pleading in connection with a small section of employment to affect the entire economy by action which would lead to an extraordinary increase in costs of production and prices.

The French and United States Government members and the Workers' members opposed the amendment on the ground that the principles involved should not be compromised and should come before national economic interests. The Brazilian Government member opposed the amendment as tending to nullify the principle of equal remuneration. The amendment was rejected by 33 votes to 39 with 2 abstentions.

The Canadian Government member, supported by the New Zealand and Swiss Government members, proposed the following amendment to replace point 4 of the Office text :

Each Member to take all practicable measures, by means appropriate to the methods of determining rates of remuneration which are in force in the country, to encourage the application of the principle of equal remuneration for men and women workers for work of equal value to all workers.

This amendment was designed to take into account the situation of Governments which, while approving the principle of equal remuneration, did not contemplate introducing legislation in the matter but were disposed to employ all other available means to promote the application of equal remuneration. The Australian Government member preferred this amendment to the Office text because he believed that application by means of collective agreements, as provided in the latter, would raise difficulties for certain Governments. The French Government member opposed the amendment and preferred the Office text which, in his opinion, provided a choice between methods of application, together with freedom to apply the principle gradually. The Workers' members also opposed the amendment because they felt that it imposed less strict obligations than the Office text on non-federal countries. The Israeli Government member proposed to modify the Canadian Government member's amendment by deleting the words " to encourage " and replacing them by the phrase " to further, and in so far as this is in conformity with the above methods, to ensure". The Canadian Government member accepted this proposal, which was supported by the Swiss Government member and the Workers' members. The Canadian Government member's amendment, as thus amended, was adopted by the Committee, subject to review by the Drafting Committee. The United States Government member then withdrew an amendment which had suggested adding the words " in accordance with Part III " after the words " to undertake " in the first line.

Point 4, as amended, was then adopted by the Committee.

Point 5

The text proposed by the Office read as follows :

5. Provision to be made that effect to the international regulation might be given by—

(a) laws or regulations ;

(b) collective agreements between employers and workers ; or

(c) a combination of laws or regulations and collective agreements between employers and workers.

The United Kingdom Government member presented an amendment to suppress point 5 but offered to withdraw this amendment if the Canadian Government member's proposal to replace the first two lines of point 5 by—

Application of the principle of equal remuneration for men and women workers for work of equal value to be sought through . . .

was modified by deleting the words " sought through " and replacing them with " by means of ". This suggestion was accepted by the Canadian Government member and the United Kingdom Government member's amendment was withdrawn.

The Australian and New Zealand Government members, together with the Workers' members, supported the Canadian Government member's amendment, as thus modified, and the amendment was adopted by 48 votes to 30 with 4 abstentions.

Point 5 of the Office text, as amended, was then adopted by the Committee.

In reply to a question by the United States Government member, the Chairman noted that the intention of both the Office text and the amendment was to give to Governments the opportunity to choose between methods of application of the principle of equal remuneration.

Replying to the Australian Government member, the Representative of the Secretary-General explained that the term "laws and regulations ", as used by the International Labour Organisation, included arbitration court decisions which had the force of law.

Point 6

The text proposed by the Office read as follows :

6. Appropriate measures to be taken to ensure co-operation of the competent public authorities with the employers' and workers' organisations concerned for the purpose of applying the principle of equal remuneration for men and women workers for work of equal value.

The United States Government member proposed that the word " ensure " should be replaced by the word " encourage ". This was opposed by the Workers' members, on the ground that the Office text was more positive and effective and therefore preferable. The Committee adopted this amendment by 43 votes to 31 with 2 abstentions.

The United Kingdom Government member moved an amendment to delete the words " applying the principle of equal remuneration for men and women workers for work of equal value ", and to replace them by the words " giving effect to the provisions of these regulations ".

The Australian Government member seconded this amendment, and it was adopted unanimously by the Committee.

Point 6 of the Office text, as amended, was then adopted.

The United Kingdom Employers' member then made a declaration that no commitments could be made as to the final attitude of the employers in plenary sitting. The report should make it quite clear that the Employers' members on the present Committee did not hold themselves committed by the text as adopted. The employers representing Australia, Denmark, India, Norway, Sweden, Switzerland, the United Kingdom and the Union of South Africa would abstain from voting on the text of Part II, General Principles.

III. Methods of Application

Point 7

The text proposed by the Office read as follows :

7. Appropriate action to be taken, after consultation with the workers or with representatives of the workers' organisations concerned, to ensure the application of the principle of equal remuneration for men and women workers for work of equal value to all employees of central Government departments or agencies and to encourage its application to employees of State, provincial or local government departments or agencies, where these have jurisdiction over rates of remuneration.

The United Kingdom Government member proposed replacing the Office text by the following :

Appropriate action to be taken in accordance with these regulations after consultation with the workers' organisations concerned, to apply the principle of equal remuneration for men and women workers for work of equal value to the employees of the Government.

This amendment was intended to limit the field of application of point 7 to employees for whom the central public authorities have a direct responsibility, while the employees of State, provincial or local government departments or agencies should be suitably provided for in point 8. The Indian Government member seconded this amendment. The Brazilian and United States Government members and the Workers' members opposed it in favour of the Office text which, in their opinion, permitted the difficulties raised by the United Kingdom Government member to be overcome. This amendment was rejected by 2 votes to 45 with 36 abstentions, including the abstentions of the Employers' members as previously indicated.

The United Kingdom Government member then suggested that the Office text might be modified by inserting the word " or " between " employees of State " and " provincial " and by omitting the words " or local " immediately after the word " provincial ". This proposal was opposed by the United States Government member and by the Workers' members. The Belgian Government member suggested, as a compromise, dividing point 7 into two paragraphs dealing respectively with the two categories of public employees, and the United Kingdom Government member proposed in addition to insert the phrase " in accordance with paragraph 4 of these regulations " after the word " encourage ".

The Committee adopted point 7 with these modifications, eight Employers' members as well as the Australian and New Zealand Government members abstaining on this point.

Point 8

The text proposed by the Office read as follows :

8. Appropriate action to be taken, after consultation with the representatives of the employers' and workers' organisations concerned, to ensure, as rapidly as practicable, the application of the principle of equal remuneration for men and women workers for work of equal value in all occupations, other than those mentioned in paragraph 7, in which remuneration rates are subject to statutory regulations or public control, particularly as regards—

(a) the establishment of minimum or other wage rates in industries and services where such rates are fixed under public authority ;

(b) industries and undertakings operated under public ownership or control ; and

(c) work executed under the terms of public contracts.

The United Kingdom Government member proposed replacement of this text by the following :

Appropriate action should be taken, in accordance with the terms of these regulations, to bring the provisions of the regulations to the notice of all wage and salary fixing authorities and employers' and workers' organisations concerned.

This amendment was intended to take into account the situation in countries in which the public authorities did not directly participate in the determination of wage rates fixed under statutory authority, or where rates of remuneration in the branches of employment under State control were fixed by independent collective bargaining. The United Kingdom Government member also believed that the principle that the conditions of work performed under public contracts should conform to the standards in force in the locality—a principle which had already been adopted by the Conference—should be respected. This proposal was seconded by the Indian Government member and supported by the United Kingdom Employers' member. The Australian Government member supported this amendment and suggested that since point 4 enunciated a general principle, it would be appropriate in point 8 to provide for an effective method of applying the principle and that this proposal offered one. The Belgian Government member and the United States Government member both opposed this amendment, remarking that it was a question of the public authorities requiring conformity to the general principle and not intervening in the fixing of rates of remuneration themselves. The Workers' members opposed the amendment, stating that public authorities which had accepted the obligation to apply the principle of equal remuneration should apply it in their role as employers.

The amendment was rejected by 25 votes to 46, with 6 abstentions.

The Canadian Government member proposed that the word " ensure " be replaced by the words " seek to ensure ". He stressed that paragraphs *(a)*, *(b)* and *(c)* of point 8 offered useful suggestions and would be satisfactory in a Recommendation, but that the Canadian Government was not prepared to accept them in a Convention. This proposal was seconded by the Australian Government member. The Workers' members opposed this, because it would weaken the force of the international regulation, and supported the Office text. The Israeli Government member suggested that the Office text should be retained, confining the Canadian Government member's amendment to paragraph *(c)*. He pointed out that the public authorities do not in fact exercise complete control over enterprises carrying out work under public contracts which are only temporary.

The Australian Government member supported this proposal, but in view of the opposition of the Workers' members, the Israeli Government member did not press for a vote. The Canadian Government member's amendment was rejected by 23 votes to 39 with 9 abstentions.

Point 8 of the Office text was then adopted by the Committee without amendment, 14 Employers' members and 7 Government members, including those of Australia, Canada, New Zealand, Norway and the United Kingdom, abstaining.

Point 9

The text proposed by the Office read as follows :

9. (1) Where suitable to established procedures for wage fixing, provisions to be made by legal enactment for the general application of the principle of equal remuneration for men and women workers for work of equal value.

(2) Provision to be made, however, that national laws and regulations might make specific exceptions to the scope of such legal enactment.

(3) Provision to be made that the competent public authority should take all necessary and appropriate measures to ensure that employers and workers are given full information as to such legal requirements, and, where appropriate, advice on their application.

Paragraph (1) was adopted by the Committee, eight Employers' members abstaining.

The Workers' members proposed that paragraph (2) be replaced by the following text :

(2) If the competent authority considers it impracticable to ensure the general application of this principle by such provisions, the authority may, after consultation with the organisations of employers and workers concerned, where such exist, exempt such occupations from the application of this Convention either generally or with such exceptions in respect of particular undertakings as it thinks fit.

The Indian Government member and the Philippines Government member both opposed this amendment in favour of the Office text, which seemed to them more flexible. The United Kingdom Employers' member also approved the Office text in so far as it provided for exemptions and he accepted consultation with employers' and workers' organisations as provided for in the Workers' members' proposal. The Israeli Government member had suggested qualifying the noun " organisations " by the adjective " representative ", but the Workers' members did not accept this suggestion. The Belgian Government member suggested, as a compromise, retaining paragraph (2) of the Office text with the following addition : " but such exceptions should be made only after consultation with the workers' and employers' organisations concerned ". The Workers' members as well as the Brazilian, French and Italian Government members accepted this proposal. The Committee adopted paragraph (2), referring it to the Drafting Committee for review, with the modification suggested by the Belgian Government member ; eight Employers' members abstained on this point.

Paragraph (3) of point 9 of the Office text was adopted unanimously.

Amendments proposed by the Workers' members to point 9 which would have been applicable to a Convention were not dealt with by the Committee in view of the decision to defer until the next session of the Conference decision on the form of the regulations.

Point 10

The text proposed by the Office read as follows :

10. When full and immediate implementation of the principle of equal remuneration for men and women workers for work of equal value should not prove feasible in the fields covered by paragraphs 7, 8 or 9, appropriate provisions to be made or caused to be made for its gradual application, by such measures as—

(a) decreasing the differentials between men's and women's wage or salary rates for work of equal value ;

(b) providing equal increments for men and women workers performing work of equal value where a system of increments is in force.

The United Kingdom Government member proposed that this text should be replaced by the following :

Where it is not practicable to give immediate effect to the principle of equal remuneration for men and women for work of equal value in the fields covered by paragraphs 7, 8 and 9, consideration be given by those responsible for the determination of remuneration to the possibility of ensuring the gradual application of this principle.

However, the United Kingdom Government member emphasised that the provisions of point 10 of the Office text, as well as those adopted in point 8, were not compatible with the principles formulated in point 4. His Government reserved the right to press at a later stage for modification to this section of the text. Meanwhile he did not propose to press this particular amendment.

The Workers' members proposed that the first part of the Office text of this point be replaced by the following :

When, after consultation with the organisations of workers and employers concerned, where such exist, it is not deemed feasible immediately to implement the principle of equal remuneration for men and women for work of equal value, then appropriate provisions to be made or caused to be made for its full application as soon as possible by such measures as—

The amendment was designed to provide for consultation between workers' and employers' organisations, which the Office text did not do, and to specify definitely that the ultimate aim was the complete application of the principle with the least possible delay.

The Committee considered first the first point contained in the amendment of the Workers' members. In order to meet objections raised by the Canadian and United Kingdom Government members, and by the Swedish Employers' members, the Workers' members agreed to insert after the words " work of equal value " the phrase " in the fields covered by paragraphs 7, 8 and 9 ". The Committee then adopted this part of the Workers' members' proposal, as amended, certain Employers' members abstaining.

The second point contained in the proposal of the Workers' members, which suggested reinforcing the Office text by specifically providing that the objective must be full application of the principle as soon as possible, was opposed by the Belgian, Indian and United States Government members and by the United States Employers' member. It was rejected by 31 votes to 39 with 6 abstentions.

The Committee adopted paragraphs *(a)* and *(b)* without change.

Point 10, as amended, was adopted, the Norwegian, Swedish and United Kingdom Government members and, as heretofore, certain Employers' members abstaining.

An amendment proposed by the Workers' members which would have been applicable to a Convention was not dealt with in view of the action of the Committee to defer until the next session of the Conference decision on the form of the regulations.

Point 11

The text proposed by the Office read as follows :

11. (1) In order to facilitate the determination of wage rates in accordance with the principle of equal remuneration for men and women workers for work of equal value, each Member, in close co-operation with the representatives of the employers' and workers' organisations concerned, to undertake or cause to be undertaken, where necessary, the establishment of methods for evaluating job content, whether by job analysis or by other procedures, with a view to providing a classification of jobs based on their various requirements, without regard to the sex of the worker.

(2) Differential rates between men and women workers which correspond to differences in job content as so determined to be considered as being in accordance with the principle of equal remuneration for men and women workers for work of equal value.

3

The Italian Employers' member proposed the deletion of paragraph (1) because he believed that the question was one of ensuring equal remuneration between men and women workers and not one of methods to be used in job analysis and job classification. The United Kingdom Employers' member seconded this proposal.

The Belgian Employers' member also supported this proposal, as well as the Italian Government member, who maintained that it was incumbent upon the workers' and employers' organisations, in the first place, to establish job classification and that the Office text appeared to be in contradiction with point 3 (2), as amended by the Committee, because it gave preference to the fixing of wage rates according to job content above all other methods. The United Kingdom Employers' member also supported this contention. The Belgian Government member opposed the amendment on the ground that the question dealt with in the paragraph directly concerned the application of the principle of equal remuneration. The amendment was rejected by 30 votes to 48 with 5 abstentions.

The French Employers' member suggested that the words " each Member, in close co-operation with the representatives of the employers' and workers' organisations concerned, to undertake or cause to be undertaken, the establishment of methods " should be replaced by the following :

... it is desirable that the employers' and workers' organisations concerned should jointly establish, when considered necessary, methods...

He believed that it was not appropriate to impose an absolute obligation to establish job classification and he felt that in addition it was the responsibility of employers' and workers' organisations to reach agreement on this point. The Italian and United Kingdom Employers' members supported this proposal. The Workers' members opposed it, preferring the Office text. The French Government member approved of the spirit of the amendment but suggested modifying the Office text as follows :

Each Member shall, at the request of employers' and workers' organisations concerned, facilitate and favour the establishment of methods for evaluating job content either by job analysis or by other means deemed appropriate.

The French Employers' member withdrew his proposal in support of this suggestion. The United States Employers' member took up again, on her own behalf, the amendment proposed by the French Employers' member, which was seconded by the Canadian Employers' member. This amendment was rejected by 37 votes to 46 with 7 abstentions.

The United Kingdom Government member, who had submitted an amendment similar to that proposed by the French Government member, withdrew it and, accepting the substance of the French Government member's proposal, suggested the following compromise text :

Where necessary and appropriate for the purpose of determining remuneration in accordance with the principle of equal remuneration for men and women workers for work of equal value, each Member, at the request of, and in co-operation with, the employers' and workers' organisations concerned, to facilitate and favour the establishment of methods for evaluating job content, either by job analysis or by other criteria deemed appropriate.

This text was accepted by the French Government and French Employers' members but opposed by the Workers' members, who preferred the Office text because the proposal of the United Kingdom Government member provided that there would have to be agreement between employers' and workers' organisations and excluded any intervention by the public authorities. The Workers' members believed that if one of the parties objected the State should intervene in order to get something done. The United States Government member also opposed this proposal. The compromise text proposed by the United Kingdom Government member was rejected by 38 votes to 47 with 6 abstentions.

An amendment proposed by the Workers' members, which suggested replacing the words " in close co-operation with " by the words " in agreement with ", was adopted by the Committee, certain Employers' members abstaining.

The Indian and United States Government members proposed replacing the phrase " where necessary " by " as far as practicable and where appropriate ". The New Zealand Workers' member opposed the use of this phrase which would weaken the Office text. The amendment was rejected by 39 votes to 42 with 6 abstentions. The Workers' members then proposed that the word " necessary " should be replaced by the word " appropriate ". This proposal was adopted by 79 votes to 2 with 5 abstentions.

The Canadian Government member then proposed that the substance of the amendment moved by the French Government member should be retained. He wished it to be made clear that, although the public authorities could render a service in promoting better understanding of the various methods of determining job content, the implementation of these methods was a matter for workers and employers.

He therefore suggested adding to the end of paragraph (1) the following :

... the application of the methods developed, however, to be in conformity with the principle of paragraph 5.

This proposal was supported by the United Kingdom Government member and the Canadian Employers' member and was adopted without opposition by the Committee.

The Workers' members proposed the suppression of paragraph (2), because this provision seemed to them to be superfluous. This amendment was rejected by 40 votes to 42 with 6 abstentions.

Point 11, as amended, was adopted by the Committee, certain Employers' members abstaining.

Point 12

The text proposed by the Office read as follows :

12. In order to facilitate the application of the principle of equal remuneration for men and women workers for work of equal value, appropriate action to be taken to raise, where necessary, the productive efficiency and capacity of women and to limit the effects of the factors accounting for the relatively low level of the remuneration of women workers, by such measures as—

(a) ensuring that workers of both sexes have equal or equivalent facilities for vocational guidance or employment counselling, vocational training and placement ;

(b) taking appropriate measures to encourage women to use facilities for vocational guidance or employment counselling, vocational training and placement ;

(c) providing welfare and social services which meet the needs of women workers, particularly those with family responsibilities, and which are financed from public funds and/or from industrial welfare funds covering all workers ; and

(d) promoting, without prejudice to the provisions of the international labour Conventions and Recommendations and national laws and regulations concerning the employment of women, equality of men and women workers as regards access to the various occupations and posts.

The Indian Government member proposed that the words " appropriate action to be taken to raise, where necessary, " be replaced by the words " States Members, at their discretion, to take appropriate action to raise ".

This proposal was seconded by the Indonesian Government member. The Belgian, New Zealand and United States Government members objected to the expression " at their discretion " and considered that the Office text was sufficiently flexible. The Indian Government member contended that States Members should not be placed under an obligation to take the measures in question, which should be left to their discretion. However, he withdrew his proposal.

The United States Government member proposed that the words " which are financed " in paragraph *(c)* should be replaced by the words " financing such services ". This proposal, seconded by the Canadian Government member, was adopted by the Committee, the New Zealand Government member abstaining. The Swiss Government member specified that the words " which are financed" should not be interpreted in the sense that social services would be financed exclusively by public grants.

Point 12, as amended, was adopted by the Committee, with the abstention of certain Employers' members.

Point 13

The text proposed by the Office read as follows :

13. In view of the importance of appraising objectively the position of the problem in the country concerned—

(a) every effort to be made to promote public understanding of the equity and usefulness of the principle of equal remuneration for men and women workers for work of equal value ; and

(b) such investigations as may be desirable to be undertaken with a view to ensuring the application of the principle.

The Indian Government member proposed the deletion of paragraph *(b)*. He did not consider it desirable to oblige States Members to undertake enquiries in the matter, because certain Governments were not in a position to meet this obligation. It would be sufficient to suggest this to States Members independently. The Swedish Employers' member, on behalf of several other Employers' members, proposed the deletion of the whole of point 13. The Belgian Government member and the Workers' members opposed this suggestion in favour of the Office text.

Paragraph *(a)* was adopted by 51 votes to 28 with 10 abstentions, and paragraph *(b)* was also retained by 49 votes to 32 with 7 abstentions.

The Canadian Government member had proposed that the word " ensuring " in the last line of point 13 of the English text be replaced by the word " encouraging ", but later he modified this suggestion by proposing that " ensuring " should be deleted and not replaced. The Indian and Israeli Government members seconded the latter proposal, which was adopted by the Committee.

Point 13, as amended, was adopted by the Committee with the abstention of certain Employers' members.

The proposed conclusions and the proposed Resolution adopted by the Committee are appended hereto.

Geneva, 27 June 1950.

(Signed) GUILDHAUME MYRDDIN-EVANS,
Chairman.

FRIEDA MILLER,
Reporter.

APPENDIX

PROPOSED CONCLUSIONS

Conclusions relating to International Regulations concerning Equal Remuneration for Men and Women Workers for Work of Equal Value

I. FORM OF THE INTERNATIONAL REGULATIONS

The form of the international regulations to be decided by the Conference at its Thirty-fourth Session.

II. GENERAL PRINCIPLES

1. For the purpose of these regulations, the term " remuneration " to be defined as including the rate of—

(a) the ordinary, basic or minimum wage or salary ; and

(b) any additional emoluments whatsoever, either in cash or in kind, which are received by the worker from his employer and arise out of his employment.

2. (1) For the purpose of these regulations, the term " equal remuneration for men and women workers for work of equal

value " to be regarded as meaning that rates of remuneration be established without discrimination based on sex.

(2) Where necessary and appropriate for this purpose, measures to be taken to promote objective appraisal of jobs on the basis of job content or, if more suitable, on any other basis as may be decided by the competent authorities or bodies responsible for the determination of remuneration, or, where the remuneration of the workers concerned is determined under collective agreements, by the parties to such agreements.

3. Each Member to take all practicable measures, by means appropriate to the methods which are in force in the country for determining rates of remuneration, to further and, in so far as this is in conformity with such methods, to ensure the application to all workers of the principle of equal remuneration for men and women workers for work of equal value.

4. Application of the principle of equal remuneration for men and women workers for work of equal value to be by means of—

(a) national laws or regulations ;

(b) collective agreements between employers and workers ; or

(c) a combination of laws or regulations and collective agreements between employers and workers.

5. Appropriate measures to be taken to encourage co-operation between the competent public authorities and the employers' and workers' organisations concerned for the purpose of giving effect to the provisions of these regulations.

III. METHODS OF APPLICATION

6. Appropriate action to be taken, after consultation with the workers or with representatives of the workers' organisations concerned—

(a) to ensure the application of the principle of equal remuneration for men and women workers for work of equal value to all employees of central Government departments or agencies, and

(b) to encourage, in accordance with paragraph 3 of these regulations, its application to employees of State, provincial or local government departments or agencies, where these have jurisdiction over rates of remuneration.

7. Appropriate action to be taken, after consultation with the representatives of the employers' and workers' organisations con-

cerned, to ensure, as rapidly as practicable, the application of the principle of equal remuneration for men and women workers for work of equal value in all occupations, other than those mentioned in paragraph 6, in which rates of remuneration are subject to statutory regulation or public control, particularly as regards—

(a) the establishment of minimum or other wage rates in industries and services where such rates are fixed under public authority ;

(b) industries and undertakings operated under public ownership or control ; and

(c) work executed under the terms of public contracts.

8. (1) Where suitable to established procedures for wage fixing, provision to be made by legal enactment for the general application of the principle of equal remuneration for men and women workers for work of equal value.

(2) National laws and regulations may make provision for specific exceptions to the scope of such legal enactment to be made after consultation with the employers' and workers' organisations concerned.

(3) Provision to be made that the competent public authority should take all necessary and appropriate measures to ensure that employers and workers are fully informed as to such legal requirements, and, where appropriate, advised on their application.

9. When, after consultation with the organisations of workers and employers concerned, where such organisations exist, it is not deemed feasible immediately to implement the principle of equal remuneration for men and women workers for work of equal value, in the fields covered by paragraphs 6, 7 and 8, appropriate provisions to be made or caused to be made for its gradual application, by such measures as—

(a) decreasing the differentials between men's and women's wage or salary rates for work of equal value ;

(b) providing equal increments for men and women workers performing work of equal value where a system of increments is in force.

10. (1) In order to facilitate the determination of wage rates in accordance with the principle of equal remuneration for men and women workers for work of equal value, each Member, in agreement with the representatives of the employers' and work-

ers' organisations concerned, to undertake or cause to be undertaken, where appropriate, the establishment of methods for evaluating job content, whether by job analysis or by other procedures, with a view to providing a classification of jobs based on their various requirements, without regard to the sex of the worker ; the application of the methods developed to be in conformity with the provisions of paragraph 4.

(2) Differential rates between men and women workers which correspond to differences in job content as so determined to be considered as being in accordance with the principle of equal remuneration for men and women workers for work of equal value.

11. In order to facilitate the application of the principle of equal remuneration for men and women workers for work of equal value, appropriate action to be taken to raise, where necessary, the productive efficiency of women workers and to limit the effects of the factors accounting for their relatively low level of remuneration by such measures as—

(a) ensuring that workers of both sexes have equal or equivalent facilities for vocational guidance or employment counselling, vocational training and placement ;

(b) taking appropriate measures to encourage women to use facilities for vocational guidance or employment counselling, vocational training and placement ;

(c) providing welfare and social services which meet the needs of women workers, particularly those with family responsibilities, and financing such services from public funds and/or from industrial welfare funds covering all workers ; and

(d) promoting, without prejudice to the provisions of international labour Conventions and Recommendations and of national laws and regulations concerning the employment of women, equality of men and women workers as regards access to occupations and posts.

12. In view of the importance of appraising objectively the position of the problem in the country concerned—

(a) every effort to be made to promote public understanding of the equity and usefulness of the principle of equal remuneration for men and women workers for work of equal value ; and

(b) such investigations as may be desirable to be undertaken with a view to the application of the principle.

Proposed Resolution concerning the Placing on the Agenda of the next Session of the Conference the Question of Equal Remuneration for Men and Women Workers for Work of Equal Value

The Conference,

Having approved the report of the Committee appointed to examine item V on its agenda,

Having in particular approved as general conclusions, with a view to the consultation of Governments, proposals for a Convention and/or a Recommendation relating to equal remuneration for men and women workers for work of equal value,

Decides to place on the agenda of its next general session the question of equal remuneration for men and women workers for work of equal value with a view to final decision on a Convention and/or a Recommendation on the subject.

Discussion in the Plenary Sitting of the Conference

The report of the Committee on Equal Remuneration came before the Conference in plenary sitting on 30 June 1950.[1]

In presenting the report, Miss Frieda Miller, United States, Government adviser and Reporter of the Committee, pointed out the wide differences in approach that had existed at the beginning of the Committee's work. It was natural and desirable that the first discussions of an area of possible international regulation should raise and fully explore all the serious questions which arose. It was natural also that problems, doubts and difficulties should be more stressed at the beginning of such a debate than the means of dealing with them. Nevertheless, the Committee had to recognise the clarifying character of the discussion and the significant progress which had been made. An outstanding characteristic of the Committee's work had been its general readiness to go forward and its constant patience and good nature in debate. Some points in the conclusions were the result of accommodation ; but others, it had been generally felt, required further study before it would be possible to arrive at a satisfactory formulation, particularly

---

[1] International Labour Conference, 33rd Session, Geneva, June 1950, *Provisional Record*, Nos. 34 and 35.

because there were important areas where reconciliation of viewpoints had yet to be secured. Thus, on the important question of the form which the principles to be enunciated should take, the decision was to be postponed until the following session. It therefore seemed particularly important for next year's Committee to have before it a full and careful analysis of each point adopted in 1950, of the relationship between each specific decision and the form and import of the other points, and of the employment of alternatives where divergencies remained.

Mr. Bergenström, Swedish Employers' delegate, speaking in the name of the employers of Denmark, Finland, Norway and Sweden, said that the subject of equal remuneration did not lend itself to international regulation for the time being, because the technical, social and economic conditions in the various countries were extremely varied. Furthermore, the wage fixing machinery prevailing in the northern countries would make it impossible for them to ratify a Convention covering wage levels. According to their experience, women's labour was more costly than men's. Women were not as capable, industrially, as men because of difficulties regarding heavy labour, higher absenteeism and lower interchangeability. The definition of equal remuneration adopted by the Committee did not take into account all these factors, which affected the cost of production. The northern employers had serious objections also to various other clauses of the text submitted by the Committee. They would therefore vote against the text and the conclusions, and would abstain from voting on the Resolution.

Mr. Kaiser, United States Government delegate, said that his Government would support the Committee's resolution to place the question of equal remuneration on the agenda of the next session of the Conference with a view to a final decision. The Government of the United States strongly supported equal remuneration for work of equal value, in policy and in practice. This policy was based upon the total experience of their country, and the United States Government, employers and workers agreed in recognising the social advantages of a high-wage, high-productivity economy. Women's work was necessary for production. Since 1870 the employment of women had increased, particularly owing to the progress of mechanisation and of mass production techniques, and they were now working in practically every occupation. " We welcome this participation in the nation's economic life ", said Mr. Kaiser, "because of the increased wealth which it puts at the disposal of our economy, but we would not welcome it at the price of a threat to wage rates or to standards of living of American workers generally." Low wage rates may drive out high ones unless counter-action were taken. In 1923 the Federal Government had set up job standards and job rates which were paid to its appointees regardless of sex ; and a large number of the States had made similar provision. On the side of management, the National Association of Manufacturers not only endorsed the principle but advised members to put it into practice and had declared that the principle was increasingly accepted by manufacturers throughout the country. As regards the trade unions, the Amalgamated Clothing Workers of America, representing 325,000 members, more than 225,000 of whom were women, had been guided throughout its 36 years' experience by the principle of equal pay for equal work, which was now thoroughly established in the men's apparel industry. The experience of the United States showed that the principle could be accepted alike by workers and employers ; that it could be translated into practice ; and that its application protected established wage rates against undercutting. Mr. Kaiser closed by pointing out that some of the problems studied by the Committee had not been solved, and that further examination was required. The double-discussion procedure had been devised for this purpose, and he was confident that a satisfactory international instrument would be put before the Conference the following year.

Mr. Hayes, Australian Workers' adviser, spoke on behalf of Mr. Vermeulen, Netherlands Workers' adviser and Workers' Vice-Chairman of the Committee. He recalled that in 1919 the Constitution of the I.L.O. had proclaimed the principle of equal remuneration, which had been confirmed in many international declarations and resolutions. The attitude of the Employers' members of the Committee had been negative. When the Committee was discussing the form of the international regulations, the Government and Workers' representatives had spoken in favour of international regulations of some sort. This meant that in the opinion of the Government representatives who spoke (and they were a large majority) as well as of the Workers' representatives it was possible to frame and introduce international regulations on the subject. In discussing the desirability of such regulations, the Workers' members had naturally considered the practical effects which they would have on the internal social and economic conditions of the countries concerned, and had therefore aimed at a text under which the proposed principles could be introduced gradually. The conclusions adopted by the Committee were sufficiently flexible to have regard to the particular conditions prevailing in the various countries. The Workers' group had explicitly stated that the principles should take the form of a Convention and that the methods of application should go into a Recommendation. The Government delegates of countries where economic and social conditions would undoubtedly undergo far-reaching changes if the principles were implemented—the United Kingdom and India, for example—had said that the adoption of international regulations, if only in the form of a Recommendation, was desirable. Other Government members had expressed the same opinion, while others again had not expressed a final view at all. Given the flexibility of the Committee's text, the Workers' group had believed that a number of these Governments would be able on further consideration to share its view and had therefore proposed that the decision regarding the form of the international regulations should be left until the next session of the Conference. An over-hasty decision could thus be avoided and the Office enabled to carry its study of the two possible forms of instrument a stage further.

Mr. Orr, Australian Employers' adviser, said that the subject of equal remuneration was not capable of international regulation but that Australian employers desired to assist in the clarification of the text, since the subject would certainly be before future sessions of the Conference. Attendance at the meetings of the Committee had only confirmed the above view. The text submitted to the Conference was not in his opinion sufficiently clear as to be internationally understood, particularly by many individuals who would need to consider and possibly act on it without having heard the discussions in committee. He would therefore vote against the majority of the conclusions.

Miss Godwin, United Kingdom Workers' adviser, pointed out that the conclusions submitted to the Conference were necessarily a compromise which had not been lightly or rapidly reached. The Workers' side recognised the importance of the question, and had approached it " in the belief that the principle of equal remuneration for work of equal value was not in doubt ... since the principle is embodied in the Constitution of the International Labour Organisation". Nevertheless, it appeared that the principle was not yet understood. It had actually been suggested that all women should be penalised for the absenteeism of some women. Absenteeism was a varying factor, among men as among women, and it had not been suggested that male workers should receive a lower rate because of absenteeism among one section of them. The rate for the job had been an accepted principle in the British trade union movement for the past sixty years. In many jobs men and women workers were completely interchangeable. The two great wars had served as a forcing ground for women's employment, and women had performed with success work traditionally reserved for men. The value of their services, in peace as in war, was not in question. The question of equal remuneration could and should be the subject of international regulations. With goodwill, difficulties of interpretation and application would fade away. The Workers' side would be jealous to preserve the principle of free wage bargaining ; but the Committee's conclusions would not involve interference with wage fixing machinery. " Whatever the difficulties may be ", said Miss Godwin, " we believe that the International Labour Organisation must meet its obligations towards women workers."

Mr. Amphlett, United Kingdom Employers' adviser, said that industry, in which he included agriculture, had primary responsibility for the standard of living in the United Kingdom, and the employers of his country had examined the question of equal remuneration with special reference to that background. They doubted whether an international regulation on the subject could be both effective and sufficiently flexible to meet the many circumstances which existed. Discussion had, however, clarified the position and exposed some of the difficulties. Though point 1 of Part II dealt with remuneration in regard to work done, remuneration was nevertheless defined in relation to employment, which was a different thing. Point 2, which aimed at defining equality of remuneration for men and women for work of equal value, could be made to mean anything the reader liked and was liable to become a bone of contention. It had been said that the principle was recognised and operated in some countries ; but these were only cases of equal remuneration as understood by the particular persons concerned. Interpretations varied, and perhaps none of them would satisfy many advocates of the principle. Did equal remuneration mean equal minimum rates, or the rate for the job, or equality of earnings, or what ? Neither the text nor the discussion in Committee clarified the matter. In the United Kingdom the rate differences between men and women in industry had been getting smaller, and there had been a wide application of the principle of " the rate for the job ". This was a normal and healthy process, which an instrument of the kind proposed would be more likely to hinder than to help. Point 2 (1) of Part II, which called for the establishment of rates of pay " without discrimination based on sex ", would put out of court nearly all the wage agreements and regulations of the United Kingdom. If the appropriate man's rate were adopted, costs of production and prices would be increased with a corresponding diminution in the general standard of living. Finally, point 10 (1) would involve Government intervention in classifying jobs. In short, United Kingdom employers doubted that the subject lent itself to international regulation, and considered that the text before them was too wide of the mark to permit of satisfactory amendment. In these circumstances they would vote against the majority of the clauses and the main text, and would abstain on the final resolution.

Miss Ebeling, United States Employers' adviser, spoke of the United States philosophy of industry. American employers felt that business should create a better life for the whole population. They looked for customers among their own employees. United States business knew that its whole purpose was service. Industry needed more women ; and women were working because they had to work. In the United States 6,500,000 families had a woman head ; 6,300,000 single women were in the labour force. This meant that over half the single women in the country had to support themselves ; and there were 18 million women working in the United States. It cost a woman who must support herself or her family just as much to live as a man. Mass production industry made sense in the United States only in so far as everybody shared in the advancing standard of life. It had been found in the United States that productivity did not depend on the sex of the worker. Remuneration could be defined as " the total inducement and rewards given by the employer to the employee for the latter's work potential, delivered in hours of work performed. In principle, remuneration is given uniformly for all human effort, without regard to sex, to all individuals whose work potential is applied to tasks with identical effectiveness." Nations of the American continent tended to claim no disparity as to sex and tried to follow the principle of uniform remuneration on the basis of proved performance. In the United States, the entrance of large numbers of women workers into war industries had accelerated the movement for paying women the rate for the job ;

in many companies women had been hired for the first time and no separate wage scale had ever been established.　In plants where differentials existed, they had often been voluntarily abolished by the employer, who recognised that the production performance of the women employed was equal and in many cases superior to that of male employees.

On 24 April 1942 the National Association of Manufacturers and the United States Chamber of Commerce had made the following statement : " There is little difference between men and women as regards their satisfactory work in industry.　Sound employment and personnel practices are applicable to both men and women and no emphasis should be placed on any distinctions between them as workers.　In the matter of wage policies we advocate the principle of equal pay for equal performance of work."

There was a threefold reason for this policy.　First, it was a matter of simple justice to pay to the person who did the job the rate which the job was worth ; second, good employee relations could not long be maintained if two employees did the same work but were unequally paid ; third, it was good management to eliminate inconsistencies in wage rates and to administer the wage schedule equitably to men and women alike.　In acting thus, United States employers were simply applying general business principles and good management, for women were important as purchasers and as sellers of goods.　Nevertheless, United States employers considered that the text before the Conference reflected conflicting ideologies and was not a well-integrated statement of principle.　They particularly objected to Part II, point 5 ; Part III, points 10 (1), 11 *(c)* and 12 *(b)*.　They considered that the question of equal remuneration should be examined at the next session of the Conference, to which alternative texts for a Convention and a Recommendation should be submitted. Furthermore, since public opinion was not yet such that the principle of equal remuneration could be followed without prejudice, it should be expressed in the form of a Recommendation.

Mr. Catin, French Employers' adviser, said that, while unable to approve the practical means by which equality of remuneration had been achieved in France, French employers did not object to the principle itself and wished it to be generally introduced in every country.　Nevertheless he could not accept the text now submitted, for two reasons.　First of all, although it was essential to give a precise definition of the words " work of equal value ", the Committee had not come near doing so ; it had not even been able to agree on the meaning of the English term " job content " and had therefore not been able to translate this in a satisfactory way. A text which remained so vague on a fundamental point was not acceptable. Secondly, the provisions of point 10 (1) might enable Governments to intervene in wage classification in a manner to which French employers would object. He would therefore vote against the conclusions as a whole, but in favour of the Resolution to retain the question on the agenda of the 34th Session of the Conference, in the hope that next year they would be able to find a text acceptable to all.

Mr. Bouladoux, French Workers' adviser, pointed out that although the principle of equal remuneration was very widely supported, few problems had moved more slowly towards a solution. Part XIII of the Treaty of Versailles mentioned equal remuneration for work of equal value, without distinction of sex, as a requirement of social justice. The principle of equal pay marked a stage in the development of our civilisation and yet, despite the great interest shown in the matter and the almost unanimous acceptance of the principle, bitter discussion had arisen regarding practical measures of secondary importance as soon as there was any question of making the principle a real and living thing. The Universal Declaration of Human Rights proclaimed that all men and women were equal in rights and dignity, and therefore equal pay must certainly be regarded as due for equal work. Furthermore, there had been in recent years a more marked tendency to determine wages objectively, to the exclusion of all personal considerations. The economic value of a given job was affected by personal effort only, and in this regard the sex of the person who made the effort was clearly quite irrelevant. Fair wages could be neither masculine nor feminine, but simply the " wage for the job ".

Mr. Bouladoux then discussed certain arguments against the application of the principle. Even if women's output were lower than that of men, the fact would be irrelevant to the problem of equal pay, since no one had asked that it be given for unequal work. Moreover, experience in some countries had to a large extent demolished arguments such as the inferior adaptability and interchangeability of women workers. During the war, women had been called upon to do jobs which had formerly been entirely or partially reserved for men, and many such women had remained in those same jobs after the war. The inequality

4

between men's and women's wages which still subsisted was perhaps due to a large extent to insufficient participation by women in the trade union movement. This was certainly not the case in the speaker's country, nor in his organisation ; but their conditions could be used as a supplementary argument, since in France, where the women workers were highly organised and were active members of the unions, the principle of equal pay for equal work was applied. Arguments of principle and arguments of fact indicated that it was fair and opportune to adopt regulations securing equality of pay. Mr. Bouladoux concluded by supporting the policy of the Workers' group with regard to the form of the future international regulations, and its proposal to adjourn decision on this point until the following year.

Mrs. Leivo-Larsson, Finnish Government delegate, pointed out that the Committee on Equal Remuneration had not taken a decision regarding the form of the international regulations, and expressed her satisfaction, having regard to the position taken by the Government of Finland, that the question was still open. Although from [the point of view of the women of the world it might appear unfortunate that the problem had not been settled in a manner satisfactory to the parties concerned, the attitude of the Committee was perhaps not as unfavourable as it might appear. Indeed the fact that the question of equal pay had been discussed within the International Labour Organisation was already proof that special attention had been devoted to it. Various views on the problem had been expressed by the Employers' and Workers' representatives ; and Government delegates had also stated their opinions. At the Conference in 1951, Governments, Employers and Workers would have a further opportunity to discuss the question and to submit their views ; the proceedings of the Committee would thus enable certain difficulties to be cleared up. It was important to settle the question of equal remuneration, for it had an important bearing on the wage problem in general, as well as on vocational training for women. Equal remuneration was likely to influence women as regards their sense of responsibility and general attitude towards their occupation. Women felt that they were regarded as an inferior class of worker, not because they worked any less well, but because of their sex. It was the speaker's personal conviction that the decision to be taken by the I.L.O. should correspond to the hopes of women's organisations in all parts of the world. It was preferable to defer decision until the following year, since it had not yet been possible to reach a satisfactory solution. Certain of the principles adopted by the Committee might facilitate practical application of the principle of equal remuneration. There had been agreement on the principle of equal pay for men and women when they do equal work ; this was itself a step forward, for in some countries it was believed that men should be paid at higher rates because they are effectively or potentially the mainstay of a family. It had also been maintained that wages should be determined on the basis of actual work only, and that social and family benefits should come from other sources, particularly since men were not the only people who had dependants. It had been stated further that a number of other factors in the different countries should also be taken into consideration, such as the economic and social status of women and the relations between workers' and employers' organisations on the one hand and governmental authorities on the other ; the appropriate action to ensure equal pay for women would depend to some extent on these factors. Despite the complexity of the problem, which had become evident during the work of the Committee, it should be solved in such a way as to meet the desire for justice felt by men and women.

Mr. Tennant, United Kingdom Government adviser, said that his Government was ready to see the Conference adopt the Committee's report. This did not mean that it regarded the conclusions as wholly satisfactory in their present form. In fact, these conclusions presented a number of serious difficulties which the United Kingdom Government hoped to see further considered and resolved before the proposed regulations were finally adopted. However, after much hard and useful work and a good deal of compromise, the Committee had submitted conclusions which the United Kingdom Government was ready to see go forward from the Conference as a basis for further consultation with Governments and preparation for the discussions next year.

The report of the Committee having been adopted without opposition, a vote by show of hands was taken on the conclusions submitted by it. These were adopted by 95 votes to 15.

A record vote was then taken on the Resolution to place on the agenda of the next general session of the Conference the question of equal remuneration for men and women workers for work of equal value ; this was adopted by 117 votes to nil with 21 abstentions.

CHAPTER II

PROPOSED TEXTS

The International Labour Conference took no decision as to the form of the international regulations concerning equal remuneration for men and women workers for work of equal value. It did, however, request the Office to prepare, on the basis of the conclusions reached by the Conference after the first discussion of the question : (1) a proposed Convention including Part II (General Principles) of these conclusions, and a proposed Recommendation including supplementary provisions, covering Part III (Methods of Application) ; and (2) a proposed general Recommendation including the provisions concerning both the General Principles and the Methods of Application. These proposed international instruments concerning equal remuneration for men and women for work of equal value will be found below, as well as the observations that they call for since, in addition to the required formal changes, certain modifications have been made to the conclusions of the Conference.

In accordance with Article 39, paragraph 6, of the Standing Orders of the Conference, Governments are asked to inform the International Labour Office not later than 15 December 1950 whether they have any amendments to suggest or comments to make.

I

A. Proposed Convention concerning Equal Remuneration for Men and Women Workers for Work of Equal Value

In Article 1, paragraph *(a)*, of the proposed Convention the words " the rate of " have been deleted since the purpose of this Article is to provide a definition of the term " remuneration " ; and paragraph *(b)* makes it clear that the principle of equal remuneration is to apply to " rates of remuneration ".

In drafting the proposed Articles, three substantial amendments have been made to paragraph 2 of the conclusions adopted by the Conference. In the first place the last part of subparagraph (1) has been modified to read " refers to rates of remuneration established without discrimination based on sex ", because the original text seemed inconsistent with the intention of this subparagraph, which is to define the expression in question and not to lay down an obligation, which is provided for in Article 2. Since, also, this is a definition of the terms used, paragraph 2 (1) has become Article 1 *(b)* in the proposed Convention. Secondly, it appeared that subparagraph (2) formulated a method of application which was considered by the Conference as fundamental, but was not intended essentially, like clause (1), to clarify the concept of equal remuneration for men and women workers for work of equal value. Subparagraph (2) has therefore been separated from Article 2 to become a new Article. It seemed appropriate to introduce it after Article 2, which stipulates that States Members shall undertake to further and, in certain conditions, to ensure the application of the principle. Thirdly, it will be recalled that the Conference was not satisfied by the French and Spanish translations of the term " job content " and requested the Office to endeavour to formulate a sufficiently clear definition of this term, so that in future an accurate translation might be made. Having rejected the French translation *nature du travail*, the Committee on Equal Remuneration adopted provisionally the French expression *caractéristiques de l'emploi*. Paragraph 2 (2), in fact, was intended to promote the establishment of methods of objective appraisal of jobs on the basis of certain criteria, one of which, explicitly provided for and defined as " job content ", excluded all considerations extraneous to the job itself. It seems, therefore, that the text could be amended to read " to promote objective appraisal of jobs on the basis of the work to be performed and the abilities required for its performance ", which would reflect accurately the intention of the original text. This proposed interpretation of the term " job content " has been introduced instead of the term itself, in both the English and French texts of the proposed Convention. In addition, the words " rates of " have been inserted before the word " remuneration ", because the obligations of the Convention apply to rates of remuneration and not to total remuneration or earnings, and the latter part of the paragraph has been redrafted with a view to clarity and brevity without change in substance.

Paragraphs 3 and 4 of the conclusions then become paragraphs 1 and 2 of Article 2 and paragraph 5 becomes Article 4 of the proposed Convention. In paragraph 5 of the conclusions, the words " between the competent public authorities and " are deleted and the word " with " is inserted, since it is clear that any obligation to encourage co-operation set forth in international regulations must be laid upon the States Members concerned.

Finally, certain additional minor changes have been made in both the English and French texts of the conclusions either to improve the drafting or to bring the texts in the two languages into conformity without, however, altering the substance of the provisions.

B. Proposed Recommendation Supplementing the Proposed Convention concerning Equal Remuneration for Men and Women Workers for Work of Equal Value

The preamble of this proposed Recommendation is not based on a decision of the Conference. It is submitted, however, in order to indicate explicitly the relationship existing between this proposed international instrument and the proposed Convention, to emphasise one of the basic principles underlying its provisions and to formulate one of the constitutional means of controlling the action taken in accordance with the recommendations adopted by the International Labour Conference.

The phrase " subject to the provisions of Article 2 of the Convention " has been included in the preamble, in order to emphasise that the means for applying the principle in the fields specified in all subsequent paragraphs of the Recommendation should conform to the methods in force for determining remuneration as provided in the Convention. The phrase has therefore been removed from the subsequent paragraphs.

The numbering of the points adopted by the Committee has been necessarily changed : former point 6 has become paragraph 1 of the new text, point 7 has become paragraph 2, and so on.

In paragraph 2, subparagraph (c), the words " where appropriate " have been included in order to meet the objections put forward by some Government members who emphasised, in particular, that the principle should be respected that the conditions of work performed under public contracts should conform to the standards in force in the locality, and that in some countries public authorities do not in fact exercise complete control over undertakings carrying out work under public contracts which are temporary in character.

In paragraph 3, subparagraph (1), the French text has been modified by replacing the word *méthodes* by the word *systèmes*, which seemed a more accurate equivalent of the English word

" procedures ". Also in this subparagraph and in subparagraph (1) of paragraph 5, the word " wage " has been replaced by the term " rates of remuneration " in accordance with the provisions of Articles 1 and 2 of the proposed Convention.

Paragraph 5 has been considerably amended. It will be recalled that the corresponding point in the conclusions (point 10) had raised a number of difficulties, since it seemed to allow an intervention of public authorities in the classification of jobs, and thus might be inconsistent with the principle formulated in Article 2 of the proposed Convention. It was therefore considered that the text should be clarified in order to avoid such a contradiction. The words " cause to be undertaken " were, consequently, replaced by the word " encourage ". Moreover, in so far as the definition of the expression " job content " as employed in Article 3 of the proposed Convention reflects the wishes of the Conference, it seems that the paragraph might be further clarified by modifying the latter part of subparagraph (1) to read : " each Member should, in agreement with the representatives of the employers' and workers' organisations concerned, establish, or encourage the establishment of, methods for objective appraisal of the work to be performed and of the abilities required for its performance, whether by job analysis or by other procedures with a view to providing a classification of jobs without regard to the sex of the worker ". The words " where appropriate " have been transferred to the beginning of the paragraph. The text thus provides that, where such methods appear appropriate, public authorities shall establish the said methods in agreement with the representatives of the employers' and workers' organisations concerned. On the other hand, public authorities, when they are not in position to intervene directly, are encouraged to promote, without exceeding the powers conferred upon them by law, the establishment of these methods and are thus invited to further measures which appear desirable. The text thus guarantees that the intervention of public authorities shall be consistent with the spirit and the letter of the procedures used in the country for the fixing of wages.

Finally, reference in this subparagraph to paragraph 4 of the conclusions has been omitted in view of the inclusive reference, in the operative clause of the preamble, to Article 2 of the Convention, in which this paragraph has now been incorporated.

In paragraph 6, subparagraph *(c)*, in order to meet the objection raised by the Swiss Government Member in committee, the

term " public funds " has been expanded to make more explicit
the types of funds which may be used for such services without
leading to wage discrimination between men and women workers.
The phrase has been modified to read " from general public funds,
social security funds and from industrial welfare funds covering
workers irrespective of sex ".

The initial phrase of paragraph 7 has been amended because
the formula adopted by the Committee referred only, to subparagraph *(b)*. The expression " appraising objectively the position of the problem in the country concerned " has been replaced
by " an informed public opinion ", in order to emphasise the primary object of this paragraph.

Finally, slight changes have been made in the English and
French texts of the conclusions which form the basis of this proposed Recommendation, either to improve the drafting or to make
the texts in both languages agree, without, however, altering the
substance of the provisions.

II

PROPOSED RECOMMENDATION CONCERNING EQUAL REMUNERATION
FOR MEN AND WOMEN WORKERS FOR WORK OF EQUAL VALUE

The provisions of this proposed text reflect exactly, but for the
unavoidable drafting changes, the corresponding provisions of the
proposed Convention and supplementary Recommendation. With
the exception of paragraph 9 (1), references to paragraph 2 have
been omitted as being cumbersome and unnecessary in a single
instrument.

I. Texts for Consideration by the Conference Should it Decide to Adopt a Convention Supplemented by a Recommendation

A. PROPOSED CONVENTION CONCERNING EQUAL REMUNERATION
FOR MEN AND WOMEN WORKERS FOR WORK OF EQUAL VALUE

The General Conference of the International Labour Organisation,

Having been convened at   by the Governing Body
    of the International Labour Office, and having met in its
    Thirty-fourth Session on   1951, and

Having decided upon the adoption of certain proposals with regard to the principle of equal remuneration for men and women workers for work of equal value, which is included in the seventh item on the agenda of the session, and

Having determined that these proposals shall take the form of an international Convention,

adopts this   day of   of the year one thousand nine hundred and fifty-one the following Convention, which may be cited as the Equal Remuneration Convention, 1951 :

Article 1

For the purpose of this Convention—

(a) the term " remuneration " includes the ordinary, basic or minimum wage or salary and any additional emoluments whatsoever, either in cash or in kind, which are received by the worker from his employer and arise out of his employment ;

(b) the term " equal remuneration for men and women workers for work of equal value " refers to rates of remuneration established without discrimination based on sex.

Article 2

1. Each Member shall take all practicable measures, by means appropriate to the methods in force for determining rates of remuneration, to further and, in so far as is in conformity with such methods, to ensure the application to all workers of the principle of equal remuneration for men and women workers for work of equal value.

2. This principle shall be applied by means of—

(a) national laws or regulations ;

(b) collective agreements between employers and workers ; or

(c) a combination of laws and regulations and collective agreements between employers and workers.

Article 3

Where necessary and appropriate, measures shall be taken to promote objective appraisal of jobs on the basis of the work to be performed and the abilities required for its performance, or on such other basis as may be decided upon by the authorities responsible for the determination of rates of remuneration or, where such rates are determined by collective agreement, by the parties thereto.

Article 4

Appropriate measures shall be taken to encourage co-operation with the employers' and workers' organisations concerned for the purpose of giving effect to the provisions of this Convention.

B. Proposed Recommendation concerning Equal Remuneration for Men and Women Workers for Work of Equal Value

The General Conference of the International Labour Organisation,

Having been convened at   by the Governing Body of the International Labour Office, and having met in its Thirty-fourth Session on   1951, and

Having decided upon the adoption of certain proposals with regard to equal remuneration for men and women workers for work of equal value, which is included in the seventh item on the agenda of the session, and

Having determined that these proposals shall take the form of a Recommendation supplementing the Equal Remuneration Convention, 1951,

adopts this   day of   of the year one thousand nine hundred and fifty-one the following Recommendation, which may be cited as the Equal Remuneration Recommendation, 1951 :

Whereas the Equal Remuneration Convention, 1951, lays down the general principle of equal remuneration for men and women workers for work of equal value ;

Whereas it is important that the methods of application of this principle should be consistent with the methods for the fixing of remuneration in use in the countries or occupations concerned ;

Whereas it is desirable to make known to all Members methods which have been found to give satisfactory results in certain countries ;

The Conference recommends that each Member should, subject to the provisions of Article 2 of the Convention, apply the following provisions, as rapidly as national conditions allow, and report to the International Labour Office as requested by the Governing Body concerning the measures taken to give effect thereto.

1. Appropriate action should be taken, after consultation with the workers or with representatives of the workers' organisations concerned—

(a) to ensure the application of the principle of equal remuneration for men and women workers for work of equal value to all employees of central government departments or agencies ; and

(b) to encourage the application of the principle to employees of State, provincial or local government departments or agencies, where these have jurisdiction over rates of remuneration.

2. Appropriate action should be taken, after consultation with the representatives of the employers' and workers' organisations concerned, to ensure, as rapidly as practicable, the application of the principle of equal remuneration for men and women workers for work of equal value in all occupations, other than those mentioned in Paragraph 1, in which rates of remuneration are subject to statutory regulation or public control, particularly as regards—

(a) the establishment of minimum or other wage rates in industries and services where such rates are fixed under public authority ;

(b) industries and undertakings operated under public ownership or control ; and

(c) where appropriate, work executed under the terms of public contracts.

3. (1) Where appropriate in the light of established procedures for the fixing of rates of remuneration, provision should be made by legal enactment for the general application of the principle of equal remuneration for men and women workers for work of equal value.

(2) National laws and regulations might make provision for specific exceptions to the scope of such legal enactment to be made after consultation with the employers' and workers' organisations concerned.

(3) The competent public authority should take all necessary and appropriate measures to ensure that employers and workers are fully informed as to such legal requirements and, where appropriate, advised on their application.

4. When, after consultation with the organisations of workers and employers concerned, where such organisations exist, it is not deemed feasible to implement immediately the principle of equal remuneration for men and women workers for work of equal value, in respect of employment covered by Paragraphs 1, 2 and 3, appropriate provision should be made, or caused to be made, for its gradual application, by such measures as—

(a) decreasing the differentials between rates of remuneration for men and rates of remuneration for women for work of equal value ;

(b) where a system of increments is in force, providing equal increments for men and women workers performing work of equal value.

5. (1) Where appropriate for the purpose of facilitating the determination of rates of remuneration in accordance with the principle of equal remuneration for men and women workers for work of equal value, each Member should, in agreement with the representatives of the employers' and workers' organisations concerned, establish or encourage the establishment of methods

for objective appraisal of the work to be performed and of the abilities required for its performance, whether by job analysis or by other procedures, with a view to providing a classification of jobs without regard to the sex of the worker.

(2) Differential rates between men and women workers which correspond to differences, as so determined, in the work to be performed and in the abilities required for its performance should be considered as being in accordance with the principle of equal remuneration for men and women workers for work of equal value.

6. In order to facilitate the application of the principle of equal remuneration for men and women workers for work of equal value, appropriate action should be taken, where necessary, to raise the productive efficiency of women workers and to limit the effects of the factors accounting for their relatively low level of remuneration, by such measures as—

(a) ensuring that workers of both sexes have equal or equivalent facilities for vocational guidance or employment counselling, vocational training and placement ;

(b) taking appropriate measures to encourage women to use facilities for vocational guidance, employment counselling, vocational training and placement ;

(c) providing welfare and social services which meet the needs of women workers, particularly those with family responsibilities, and financing such services from general public funds or social security funds or industrial welfare funds covering workers irrespective of sex ; and

(d) promoting, without prejudice to the provisions of international labour Conventions and Recommendations and of national laws and regulations concerning the employment of women, equality of men and women workers as regards access to occupations and posts.

7. In view of the importance of an informed public opinion—

(a) every effort should be made to promote public understanding of the equity and usefulness of the principle of equal remuneration for men and women workers for work of equal value ; and

(b) such investigations as may be desirable to promote the application of the principle should be undertaken.

II. Text for Consideration by the Conference
Should it Decide to Adopt a Recommendation Alone

PROPOSED RECOMMENDATION CONCERNING EQUAL REMUNERATION
FOR MEN AND WOMEN WORKERS FOR WORK OF EQUAL VALUE

The General Conference of the International Labour Organisation,

Having been convened at   by the Governing Body
of the International Labour Office, and having met in its
Thirty-fourth Session on   1951, and

Having decided upon the adoption of certain proposals with
regard to equal remuneration for men and women workers
for work of equal value, which is the seventh item on the
agenda of the session, and

Having determined that these proposals shall take the form
of a Recommendation,

adopts this   day of   of the year one thousand nine
hundred and fifty-one the following Recommendation, which may
be cited as the Equal Remuneration Recommendation, 1951 :

I. *General Principles*

1. For the purpose of this Recommendation—

(a) the term " remuneration " includes the ordinary basic or
minimum wage or salary, and any additional emoluments
whatsoever, either in cash or in kind, which are received
by the worker from his employer and arise out of his employment ;

(b) the term " equal remuneration for men and women workers
for work of equal value " refers to rates of remuneration
established without discrimination based on sex.

2. (1) Each Member should take all practicable measures, by
means which are appropriate to the methods in force for determining rates of remuneration, to further and, in so far as is in
conformity with such methods, to ensure the application to all
workers of the principle of equal remuneration for men and women
workers for work of equal value.

(2) This principle should be applied by means of—

(a) national laws or regulations ;

(b) collective agreements between employers and workers ;

(c) a combination of laws or regulations and collective agreements between employers and workers.

3. Where necessary and appropriate for this purpose, measures
should be taken to promote objective appraisal of jobs on the basis

of the work to be performed and of the abilities required for its performance, or on such other basis as may be decided upon by the authorities responsible for the determination of rates of remuneration or, where such rates are determined under collective agreement, by the parties to such agreement.

4. Appropriate measures should be taken to encourage co-operation with the employers' and workers' organisations concerned for the purpose of giving effect to the provisions of this Recommendation.

II. *Methods of Application*

5. Appropriate action should be taken, after consultation with the workers or with representatives of the workers' organisations concerned—

(a) to ensure the application of the principle of equal remuneration for men and women workers for work of equal value to all employees of central government departments or agencies ; and

(b) to encourage the application of the principle to employees of State, provincial or local government departments or agencies, where these have jurisdiction over rates of remuneration.

6. Appropriate action should be taken, after consultation with the representatives of the employers' and workers' organisations concerned, to ensure, as rapidly as practicable, the application of the principle of equal remuneration for men and women workers for work of equal value in all occupations, other than those mentioned in Paragraph 5, in which rates of remuneration are subject to statutory regulation or public control, particularly as regards—

(a) the establishment of minimum or other wage rates in industries and services where such rates are fixed under public authority ;

(b) industries and undertakings operated under public ownership or control ; and

(c) where appropriate, work executed under the terms of public contracts.

7. (1) Where appropriate in the light of established procedures for the fixing of rates of remuneration, provision should be made by legal enactment for the general application of the principle of equal remuneration for men and women workers for work of equal value.

(2) National laws and regulations might provide for specific exceptions to the scope of such legal enactment to be made after consultation with the employers' and workers' organisations concerned.

(3) The competent public authority should take all necessary and appropriate measures to ensure that employers and workers

are fully informed as to such legal requirements and, where appropriate, advised on their application.

8. When, after consultation with the organisations of workers and employers concerned, where such organisations exist, it is not deemed feasible to implement immediately the principle of equal remuneration for men and women workers for work of equal value, in respect of employment covered by Paragraphs 5, 6 and 7, appropriate provision should be made, or caused to be made, for its gradual application, by such measures as—

(a) decreasing the differentials between rates of remuneration for men and rates of remuneration for women, for work of equal value ;

(b) where a system of increments is in force, providing equal increments for men and women workers performing work of equal value.

9. (1) Where appropriate for the purpose of facilitating the determination of rates of remuneration in accordance with the principle of equal remuneration for men and women workers for work of equal value, each Member should, in agreement with the representatives of the employers' and workers' organisations concerned, establish, or encourage the establishment of, methods for objective appraisal of the work to be performed and of the abilities required in its performance, whether by job analysis or by other procedures, with a view to providing a classification of jobs without regard to the sex of the worker ; such methods should be applied in accordance with the provisions of Paragraph 2 of this Recommendation.

(2) Differential rates between men and women workers which correspond to differences, as so determined, in the work to be performed and in the abilities required for its performance should be considered as being in accordance with the principle of equal remuneration for men and women workers for work of equal value.

10. In order to facilitate the application of the principle of equal remuneration for men and women workers for work of equal value, appropriate action should be taken, where necessary, to raise the productive efficiency of women workers and to limit the effects of the factors accounting for their relatively low level of remuneration, by such measures as—

(a) ensuring that workers of both sexes have equal or equivalent facilities for vocational guidance or employment counselling, vocational training and placement ;

(b) taking appropriate measures to encourage women to use facilities for vocational guidance, employment counselling, vocational training and placement ;

(c) providing welfare and social services which meet the needs of women workers, particularly those with family responsibilities, and financing such services from general public funds

or social security funds or industrial welfare funds covering workers irrespective of sex ; and

(d) promoting, without prejudice to the provisions of international labour Conventions and Recommendations and of national laws and regulations concerning the employment of women, equality of men and women workers as regards access to occupations and posts.

11. In view of the importance of an informed public opinion—

(a) every effort should be made to promote public understanding of the equity and usefulness of the principle of equal remuneration for men and women workers for work of equal value ; and

(b) such investigations as may be desirable to promote the application of the principle should be undertaken.